TURNBULL

BRITAIN IN PICTURES
THE BRITISH PEOPLE IN PICTURES

THE ENGLISH PEOPLE

GENERAL EDITOR
W. J. TURNER

The Editor is most grateful to all those who have
so kindly helped in the selection of illustrations
especially to officials of the various public
Museums Libraries and Galleries and
to all others who have generously
allowed pictures and MSS
to be reproduced

THE
ENGLISH PEOPLE

GEORGE ORWELL

*WITH
8 PLATES IN COLOUR
AND
17 ILLUSTRATIONS IN
BLACK & WHITE*

COLLINS · 14 ST. JAMES'S PLACE · LONDON
MCMXLVII

PRODUCED BY
ADPRINT LIMITED LONDON

PRINTED IN GREAT BRITAIN
BY JARROLD AND SONS LTD NORWICH
ON MELLOTEX BOOK PAPER MADE
BY TULLIS RUSSELL AND CO LTD MARKINCH SCOTLAND

LIST OF ILLUSTRATIONS

PLATES IN COLOUR

"THE GODS"
The Gallery at a London Theatre
Oil painting by Sydney Seymour-Lucas, 1942

INDUSTRIAL LANDSCAPE
The Great North Road at Castleford, South Yorkshire
Water colour by F. C. Jones, 1946

BLACK AND WHITE ILLUSTRATIONS

PICCADILLY CIRCUS, NOVEMBER 1940
Water colour by Feliks Topolski

ENGLAND AT FIRST GLANCE

IN peacetime, it is unusual for foreign visitors to this country to notice
the existence of the English people. Even the accent referred to by
Americans as "the English accent" is not in fact common to more than
a quarter of the population. In cartoons in Continental papers England is
personified by an aristocrat with a monocle, a sinister capitalist in a top hat,
or a spinster in a Burberry. Hostile or friendly, nearly all the generalisations
that are made about England base themselves on the property-owning class
and ignore the other forty-five million.

But the chances of war brought to England, either as soldiers or as
refugees, hundreds of thousands of foreigners who would not normally
have come here, and forced them into intimate contact with ordinary people.
Czechs, Poles, Germans and Frenchmen to whom "England" meant
Piccadilly and the Derby found themselves quartered in sleepy East Anglian
villages, in northern mining towns, or in the vast working-class areas of
London whose names the world had never heard until they were blitzed.

7

Those of them who had the gift of observation will have seen for themselves that the real England is not the England of the guide-books. Blackpool is more typical than Ascot, the top hat is a moth-eaten rarity, the language of the B.B.C. is barely intelligible to the masses. Even the prevailing physical type does not agree with the caricatures, for the tall, lanky physique which is traditionally English is almost confined to the upper classes: the working classes, as a rule, are rather small, with short limbs and brisk movements, and with a tendency among the women to grow dumpy in early middle life.

It is worth trying for a moment to put oneself in the position of a foreign observer, new to England, but unprejudiced, and able because of his work to keep in touch with ordinary, useful, unspectacular people. Some of his generalisations would be wrong, because he would not make enough allowance for the temporary dislocations resulting from war. Never having seen England in normal times, he might underrate the power of class distinctions, or think English agriculture healthier than it is, or be too much impressed by the dinginess of the London streets or the prevalence of drunkenness. But with his fresh eyes he would see a great deal that a native observer misses, and his probable impressions are worth tabulating. Almost certainly he would find the salient characteristics of the English common people to be artistic insensibility, gentleness, respect for legality, suspicion of foreigners, sentimentality about animals, hypocrisy, exaggerated class distinctions, and an obsession with sport.

As for our artistic insensibility, ever-growing stretches of beautiful countryside are ruined by planless building, the heavy industries are allowed to convert whole counties into blackened deserts, ancient monuments are wantonly pulled down or swamped by seas of yellow brick, attractive vistas are blocked by hideous statues to nonentities—and all this without any *popular* protest whatever. When England's housing problem is discussed, its æsthetic aspect simply does not enter the mind of the average man. Nor is there any widespread interest in any of the arts, except perhaps music. Poetry, the art in which above all others England has excelled, has for more than a century had no appeal whatever for the common people. It is only acceptable when—as in some popular songs and mnemonic rhymes—it is masquerading as something else. Indeed the very word "poetry" arouses either derision or embarrassment in ninety-eight people out of a hundred.

Our imaginary foreign observer would certainly be struck by our gentleness: by the orderly behaviour of English crowds, the lack of pushing and quarrelling, the willingness to form queues, the good temper of harassed, overworked people like bus conductors. The manners of the English working class are not always very graceful, but they are extremely considerate. Great care is taken in showing a stranger the way, blind people can travel across London with the certainty that they will be helped on and off every bus and across every street. In wartime a few of the policemen

IN THE COUNTRY
Hop Picking near Maidstone, Kent
Water colour drawing by John Minton, 1945

EVENING BY THE RIVER
Salisbury in Wartime
Water colour by Edward Ardizzone, 1940

carried revolvers, but England has nothing corresponding to the *gendarmerie*, the semi-military police living in barracks and armed with rifles (sometimes even with tanks and aeroplanes) who are the guardians of society all the way from Calais to Tokyo. And except for certain well-defined areas in half a dozen big towns there is very little crime or violence. The average of honesty is lower in the big towns than in the country, but even in London the newsvendor can safely leave his pile of pennies on the pavement while he goes for a drink. The prevailing gentleness of manners is a recent thing, however. Well within living memory it was impossible for a smartly dressed person to walk down Ratcliff Highway without being assaulted, and an eminent jurist, asked to name a typically English crime, could answer: "Kicking your wife to death."

There is no revolutionary tradition in England, and even in extremist political parties, it is only the middle-class membership that thinks in revolutionary terms. The masses still more or less assume that "against the law" is a synonym for "wrong." It is known that the criminal law is harsh and full of anomalies and that litigation is so expensive as always to favour the rich against the poor: but there is a general feeling that the law, such as it is, will be scrupulously administered, that a judge or magistrate cannot be bribed, that no one will be punished without trial. An Englishman does not believe in his bones, as a Spanish or Italian peasant does, that the law is simply a racket. It is precisely this general confidence in the law that has allowed a good deal of recent tampering with Habeas Corpus to escape public notice. But it also causes some ugly situations to end peacefully. During the worst of the London blitz the authorities tried to prevent the public from using the Tube stations as shelters. The people did not reply by storming the gates, they simply bought themselves penny-halfpenny tickets: they thus had legal status as passengers, and there was no thought of turning them out again.

The traditional English xenophobia is stronger among the working class than the middle class. It was partly the resistance of the Trade Unions that prevented a really large influx of refugees from the fascist countries before the war, and when the German refugees were interned in 1940, it was not the working class that protested. The difference in habits, and especially in food and language, makes it very hard for English working people to get on with foreigners. Their diet differs a great deal from that of any European nation, and they are extremely conservative about it. As a rule they will refuse even to sample a foreign dish, they regard such things as garlic and olive oil with disgust, life is unlivable to them unless they have tea and puddings. And the peculiarities of the English language make it almost impossible for anyone who has left school at fourteen to learn a foreign language after he has grown up. In the French Foreign Legion, for instance, the British and American legionaries seldom rise out of the ranks, because they cannot learn French, whereas a German learns French in a

9

few months. English working people, as a rule, think it effeminate even to pronounce a foreign word correctly. This is bound up with the fact that the upper classes learn foreign languages as a regular part of their education. Travelling abroad, speaking foreign tongues, enjoying foreign food, are vaguely felt to be upper-class habits, a species of snobbery, so that xenophobia is reinforced by class jealousy.

Perhaps the most horrible spectacles in England are the Dogs' Cemeteries in Kensington Gardens, at Stoke Poges (it actually adjoins the churchyard where Gray wrote his famous *Elegy*) and at various other places. But there were also the Animals' A.R.P. Centres, with miniature stretchers for cats, and in the first year of the war there was the spectacle of Animal Day being celebrated with all its usual pomp in the middle of the Dunkirk evacuation. Although its worst follies are committed by the upper-class women, the animal cult runs right through the nation and is probably bound up with the decay of agriculture and the dwindled birthrate. Several years of stringent rationing have failed to reduce the dog and cat population, and even in poor quarters of big towns the bird fanciers' shops display canary seed at prices ranging up to twenty-five shillings a pint.

Hypocrisy is so generally accepted as part of the English character that a foreign observer would be prepared to meet with it at every turn, but he would find especially ripe examples in the laws dealing with gambling, drinking, prostitution, and profanity. He would find it difficult to reconcile the anti-imperialistic sentiments which are commonly expressed in England with the size of the British Empire. If he were a continental European he would notice with ironical amusement that the English think it wicked to have a big army but see nothing wrong in having a big navy. This too he would set down as hypocrisy—not altogether fairly, for it is the fact of being an island, and therefore not needing a big army, that has allowed British democratic institutions to grow up, and the mass of the people are fairly well aware of this.

Exaggerated class distinctions have been diminishing over a period of about thirty years, and the war has probably speeded up the process, but newcomers to England are still astonished and sometimes horrified by the blatant differences between class and class. The great majority of the people can still be "placed" in an instant by their manners, clothes, and general appearance. Even the physical type differs considerably, the upper classes being on an average several inches taller than the working class. But the most striking difference of all is in language and accent. The English working class, as Mr. Wyndham Lewis has put it, are "branded on the tongue." And though class distinctions do not exactly coincide with economic distinctions, the contrast between wealth and poverty is very much more glaring, and more taken for granted, than in most countries.

The English were the inventors of several of the world's most popular games, and have spread them more widely than any other product of their

FISH QUEUE
Detail from an oil painting by Evelyn Dunbar, 1943

culture. The word "football" is mispronounced by scores of millions who have never heard of Shakespeare or Magna Charta. The English themselves are not outstandingly good at all games, but they enjoy playing them, and to an extent that strikes foreigners as childish they enjoy reading about them and betting on them. During the between-war years the football pools did more than any other one thing to make life bearable for the unemployed. Professional footballers, boxers, jockeys, and even cricketers enjoy a popularity that no scientist or artist could hope to rival. Nevertheless sport-worship is not carried to quite such imbecile lengths as one would imagine from reading the popular press. When the brilliant lightweight boxer, Kid Lewis, stood for Parliament in his native borough, he only scored a hundred and twenty-five votes.

These traits that we have enumerated are probably the ones that would strike an intelligent foreign observer first. Out of them he might feel that he could construct a reliable picture of the English character. But then probably a thought would strike him: is there such a thing as "the English character"? Can one talk about nations as though they were individuals? And supposing that one can, is there any genuine continuity between the England of to-day and the England of the past?

As he wandered through the London streets, he would notice the old prints in the bookshop windows, and it would occur to him that if these things are representative, then England must have changed a great deal. It is not much more than a hundred years since the distinguishing mark of

English life was its brutality. The common people, to judge by the prints, spent their time in an almost unending round of fighting, whoring, drunkenness, and bull-baiting. Moreover, even the physical type appears to have changed. Where are they gone, the hulking draymen and low-browed prize-fighters, the brawny sailors with their buttocks bursting out of their white trousers, and the great overblown beauties with their swelling bosoms, like the figure-heads of Nelson's ships? What had these people in common with the gentle-mannered, undemonstrative, law-abiding English of to-day? Do such things as "national cultures" really exist?

This is one of those questions, like the freedom of the will or the identity of the individual, in which all the arguments are on one side and instinctive knowledge is on the other. It is not easy to discover the connecting thread that runs through English life from the sixteenth century onwards, but all English people who bother about such subjects feel that it exists. They feel that they understand the institutions that have come to them out of the past—Parliament, for instance, or sabbatarianism, or the subtle grading of the class system—with an inherited knowledge impossible to a foreigner. Individuals, too, are felt to conform to a national pattern. D. H. Lawrence is felt to be "very English," but so is Blake; Dr. Johnson and G. K. Chesterton are somehow the same kind of person. The belief that we resemble our ancestors—that Shakespeare, say, is more like a modern Englishman than a modern Frenchman or German—may be unreasonable, but by existing it influences conduct. Myths which are believed in tend to become true, because they set up a type, or "persona," which the average person will do his best to resemble.

During the bad period of 1940 it became clear that in Britain national solidarity is stronger than class antagonism. If it were really true that "the proletarian has no country," 1940 was the time for him to show it. It was exactly then, however, that class feeling slipped into the background, only reappearing when the immediate danger had passed. Moreover, it is probable that the stolid behaviour of the British town populations under the bombing was partly due to the existence of the national "persona"—that is, to their preconceived idea of themselves. Traditionally the Englishman is phlegmatic, unimaginative, not easily rattled: and since that is what he thinks he ought to be, that is what he tends to become. Dislike of hysteria and "fuss," admiration for stubbornness, are all but universal in England, being shared by everyone except the intelligentsia. Millions of English people willingly accept as their national emblem the bulldog, an animal noted for its obstinacy, ugliness, and impenetrable stupidity. They have a remarkable readiness to admit that foreigners are more "clever" than themselves, and yet they feel that it would be an outrage against the laws of God and Nature for England to be ruled by foreigners. Our imaginary observer would notice, perhaps, that Wordsworth's sonnets during the Napoleonic war might almost have been written during this one. He would know

A DEE RIVER SALMON FISHER
Water colour by A. S. Hartrick

already that England has produced poets and scientists rather than philosophers, theologians, or pure theorists of any description. And he might end by deciding that a profound, almost unconscious patriotism and an inability to think logically are the abiding features of the English character, traceable in English literature from Shakespeare onwards.

13

THE MORAL OUTLOOK OF THE ENGLISH PEOPLE

FOR perhaps a hundred and fifty years, organised religion, or conscious religious belief of any kind, have had very little hold on the mass of the English people. Only about ten per cent of them ever go near a place of worship except to be married and buried. A vague theism and an intermittent belief in life after death are probably fairly widespread, but the main Christian doctrines have been largely forgotten. Asked what he meant by "Christianity," the average man would define it wholly in ethical terms ("unselfishness," or "loving your neighbour," would be the kind of definition he would give). This was probably much the same in the early days of the Industrial Revolution, when the old village life had been suddenly broken up and the Established Church had lost touch with its followers. But in recent times the Nonconformist sects have also lost much of their vigour, and within the last generation the Bible-reading which used to be traditional in England has lapsed. It is quite common now to meet with young people who do not know the Bible stories even as *stories*.

But there is one sense in which the English common people have remained more Christian than the upper classes, and probably than any other European nation. This is in their non-acceptance of the modern cult of power-worship. While almost ignoring the spoken doctrines of the Church, they have held on to the one that the Church never formulated, because taking it for granted: namely, that might is not right. It is here that the gulf between the intelligentsia and the common people is widest. From Carlyle onwards, but especially in the last generation, the British intelligentsia have tended to take their ideas from Europe and have been infected by habits of thought that derive ultimately from Machiavelli. All the cults that have been fashionable in the last dozen years, communism, fascism, and pacifism, are in the last analysis forms of power-worship. It is significant that in this country, unlike most others, the Marxist version of Socialism has found its warmest adherents in the middle class. Its methods, if not its theories, obviously conflict with what is called "*bourgeois* morality" (i.e., common decency), and in moral matters it is the proletarians who are "*bourgeois*."

One of the basic folk-tales of the English-speaking peoples is Jack the Giant-killer—the little man against the big man. Mickey Mouse, Popeye the Sailor, and Charlie Chaplin are all essentially the same figure. (Chaplin's films, it is worth noticing, were banned in Germany as soon as Hitler came to power, and Chaplin has been viciously attacked by English fascist writers.) Not merely a hatred of bullying, but a tendency to support the weaker side merely because it is weaker, are almost general in England. Hence the admiration for a "good loser" and the easy forgiveness of failures, either in sport, politics, or war. Even in very serious matters the English people do not feel that an unsuccessful action is necessarily futile. An

14

example in the 1939-45 war was the campaign in Greece. No one expected it to succeed, but nearly everyone thought that it should be undertaken. And the popular attitude to foreign politics is nearly always coloured by the instinct to side with the under-dog.

An obvious recent instance was pro-Finnish sentiment in the Russo-Finnish war of 1940. This was genuine enough, as several by-elections fought mainly on this issue showed. Popular feeling towards the U.S.S.R. had been increasingly friendly for some time past, but Finland was a small country attacked by a big one, and that settled the issue for most people. In the American Civil War the British working classes sided with the North—the side that stood for the abolition of slavery—in spite of the fact that the Northern blockade of the cotton ports was causing great hardship in Britain. In the Franco-Prussian war, such pro-French sentiment as there was in England was among the working class. The small nationalities oppressed by the Turks found their sympathisers in the Liberal Party, at that time the party of the working class and the lower middle class. And in so far as it bothered with such issues at all, British mass sentiment was for the Abyssinians against the Italians, for the Chinese against the Japanese, and for the Spanish Republicans against Franco. It was also friendly to Germany during the period when Germany was weak and disarmed, and it is not surprising to see a similar swing of sentiment after this war.

The feeling that one ought always to side with the weaker party probably derives from the balance-of-power policy which Britain has followed from the eighteenth century onwards. A European critic would add that it is humbug, pointing in proof to the fact that Britain herself holds down subject populations in India and elsewhere. We don't, in fact, know what settlement the English common people would make with India if the decision were theirs. All political parties and all newspapers of whatever colour have conspired to prevent them from seeing the issue clearly. We do know, however, that they have sometimes championed the weak against the strong when it was obviously not to their own advantage. The best example is the Irish Civil War. The real weapon of the Irish rebels was British public opinion, which was substantially on their side and prevented the British Government from crushing the rebellion in the only way possible. Even in the Boer War there was a considerable volume of pro-Boer sentiment, though it was not strong enough to influence events. One must conclude that in this matter the English common people have lagged behind their century. They have failed to catch up with power politics, "realism," *sacro egoismo* and the doctrine that the end justifies the means.

The general English hatred of bullying and terrorism means that any kind of violent criminal gets very little sympathy. Gangsterism on American lines could not flourish in England, and it is significant that the American gangsters have never tried to transfer their activities to this country. At need, the whole nation would combine against people who kidnap babies and fire machine-guns in the street: but even the efficiency of the English police force really depends on the fact that the police have public opinion behind them. The bad side of this is the almost universal toleration of cruel and out-of-date punishments. It is not a thing to be proud of that England should still tolerate such punishments as flogging. It continues partly because of the widespread psychological ignorance, partly because men are only flogged for crimes that forfeit nearly everyone's sympathy. There would be an outcry if it were applied to non-violent crimes, or re-instituted for military offences. Military punishments are not taken for granted in England as they are in most countries. Public opinion is almost certainly opposed to the death penalty for cowardice and desertion, though there is no strong feeling against hanging murderers. In general the English attitude to crime is ignorant and old-fashioned, and humane treatment even of child offenders is a recent thing. Still, if Al Capone were in an English jail, it would not be for evasion of income tax.

A more complex question than the English attitude to crime and violence is the survival of puritanism and the world-famed English hypocrisy.

The English people proper, the working masses who make up seventy-five per cent of the population, are not puritanical. The dismal theology of Calvinism never popularised itself in England as it did for a while in Wales and Scotland. But puritanism in the looser sense in which the word is generally used (that is, prudishness, asceticism, the "kill-joy" spirit) is something that has been unsuccessfully forced upon the working class by the class of small traders and manufacturers immediately above them. In its origin it had a clear though unconscious economic motive behind it. If you could persuade the working man that every kind of recreation was sinful, you could get more work out of him for less money. In the early nineteenth century there was even a school of thought which maintained that the working man ought not to marry. But it would be unfair to suggest that the puritan moral code was mere humbug. Its exaggerated fear of sexual immorality, which extended to a disapproval of stage plays, dancing, and even bright-coloured clothes, was partly a protest against the real corruption of the later Middle Ages: there was also the new factor of syphilis, which appeared in England about the sixteenth century and worked frightful havoc for the next century or two. A little later there was another new factor in the introduction of distilled liquors—gin, brandy, and so forth—which were very much more intoxicating than the beer and mead which the English had been accustomed to. The "temperance" movement was a well-meant reaction against the frightful drunkenness of the nineteenth century, product of slum conditions and cheap gin. But it was necessarily led by fanatics who regarded not merely drunkenness but even the moderate drinking of alcohol as sinful. During the past fifty years or so there has even been a similar drive against tobacco. A hundred years ago, or two hundred years ago, tobacco-smoking was much disapproved of,

A LONDON FAIR
The Vale of Health, Hampstead
Water colour by Dorothy Copsey, 1944

VICTORY DAY
Richmond Hill, Surrey
Oil painting by Mary Kent Harrison, 1945

but only on the ground that it was dirty, vulgar, and injurious to health: the idea that it is a wicked self-indulgence is modern.

This line of thought has never really appealed to the English masses. At most they have been sufficiently intimidated by middle-class puritanism to take some of their pleasures rather furtively. It is universally agreed that the working classes are far more moral than the upper classes, but the idea that sexuality is wicked in itself has no popular basis. Music-hall jokes, Blackpool postcards, and the songs the soldiers make up are anything but puritanical. On the other hand, almost no one in England approves of prostitution. There are several big towns where prostitution is extremely blatant, but it is completely unattractive and has never been really tolerated. It could not be regulated and humanised as it has been in some countries, because every English person feels in his bones that it is wrong. As for the general weakening of sex morals that has happened during the past twenty or thirty years, it is probably a temporary thing, resulting from the excess of women over men in the population.

In the matter of drink, the only result of a century of "temperance" agitation has been a slight increase in hypocrisy. The practical disappearance of drunkenness as an English vice has not been due to the anti-drink fanatics, but to competing amusements, education, the improvement in industrial conditions, and the expensiveness of drink itself. The fanatics have been able to see to it that the Englishman drinks his glass of beer under difficulties and with a faint feeling of wrong-doing, but have not actually been able to prevent him from drinking it. The pub, one of the basic institutions of English life, carries on in spite of the harassing tactics of Nonconformist local authorities. So also with gambling. Most forms of gambling are illegal according to the letter of the law, but they all happen on an enormous scale. The motto of the English people might be the chorus of Marie Lloyd's song, "A little of what you fancy does you good." They are not vicious, not even lazy, but they will have their bit of fun, whatever the higher-ups may say. And they seem to be gradually winning their battle against the kill-joy minorities. Even the horrors of the English Sunday have been much mitigated during the past dozen years. Some of the laws regulating pubs—designed in every case to discourage the publican and make drinking unattractive—were relaxed during the war. And it is a very good sign that the stupid rule forbidding children to enter pubs, which tended to dehumanise the pub and turn it into a mere drinking-shop, is beginning to be disregarded in some parts of the country.

Traditionally, the Englishman's home is his castle. In an age of conscription and identity cards this cannot really be true. But the hatred of regimentation, the feeling that your spare time is your own and that a man must not be persecuted for his opinions, is deeply ingrained, and the centralising processes inevitable in wartime, and still enforced, have not destroyed it.

POLITICAL MEETING, HYDE PARK CORNER
Brush and chalk drawing by Lucien Pissarro, 1863-1749

It is a fact that the much-boasted freedom of the British press is theoretical rather than actual. To begin with the centralised ownership of the press means in practice that unpopular opinons can only be printed in books or in newspapers with small circulations. Moreover, the English people as a whole are not sufficiently interested in the printed word to be very vigilant about this aspect of their liberties, and during the last twenty years there has been much tampering with the freedom of the press, with no real popular protest. Even the demonstrations against the suppression of the *Daily Worker* were probably stage-managed by a small minority. On the other hand, freedom of speech is a reality, and respect for it is almost general. Extremely few English people are afraid to utter their political opinions in public, and there are not even very many who want to silence the opinions of others. In peacetime, when unemployment can be used as a weapon, there is a certain amount of petty persecution of "reds," but the real totalitarian atmosphere, in which the State endeavours to control people's thoughts as well as their words, is hardly imaginable.

The safeguard against it is partly the respect for integrity of conscience, and the willingness to hear both sides, which can be observed at any public meeting. But it is also partly the prevailing lack of intellectuality. The English are not sufficiently interested in intellectual matters to be intolerant about them. "Deviations" and "dangerous thoughts" do not seem very important to them. An ordinary Englishman, Conservative, Socialist, Catholic,

FLYING KITES IN BATTERSEA PARK
Etching by Anthony Gross, 1934

Communist, or what not, almost never grasps the full logical implications of the creed he professes: almost always he utters heresies without noticing it. Orthodoxies, whether of the Right or the Left, flourish chiefly among the literary intelligentsia, the people who ought in theory to be the guardians of freedom of thought.

The English people are not good haters, their memory is very short, their patriotism is largely unconscious, they have no love of military glory and not much admiration for great men. They have the virtues and the vices of an old-fashioned people. To twentieth-century political theories they oppose not another theory of their own, but a moral quality which must be vaguely described as decency. On the day in 1936 when the Germans re-occupied the Rhineland I was in a northern mining town. I happened to go into a pub just after this piece of news, which quite obviously meant war, had come over the wireless, and I remarked to the others at the bar, "The German army has crossed the Rhine." With a vague air of capping a quotation someone answered, "Parley-voo." No more response than that! Nothing will ever wake these people up, I thought. But later in the evening, at the same pub, someone sang a song which had recently come out, with the chorus—

> "For you can't do that there 'ere,
> No, you can't do that there 'ere;
> Anywhere else you can do that there,
> But you can't do that there 'ere!"

And it struck me that perhaps this was the English answer to fascism. At any rate it is true that it has not happened here, in spite of fairly favourable circumstances. The amount of liberty, intellectual or other, that we enjoy in England ought not to be exaggerated, but the fact that it did not markedly diminish in nearly six years of desperate war is a hopeful symptom.

THE POLITICAL OUTLOOK OF THE ENGLISH PEOPLE

THE English people are not only indifferent to fine points of doctrine, but are remarkably ignorant politically. They are only now beginning to use the political terminology which has been current for years in Continental countries. If you asked a random group of people from any stratum of the population to define capitalism, socialism, communism, anarchism, Trotskyism, fascism, you would get mostly vague answers, and some of them would be surprisingly stupid ones.

But they are also distinctly ignorant about their own political system. During recent years, for various reasons, there has been a revival of political activity, but over a longer period the interest in party politics has been dwindling. Great numbers of adult English people have never in their lives bothered to vote in an election. In big towns it is quite common for people not to know the name of their M.P. or what constituency they live in. During the war years, owing to the failure to renew the registers, the young had no votes (at one time no one under twenty-nine had a vote), and did not seem much troubled by the fact. Nor does the anomalous electoral system, which usually favours the Conservative Party, though it happened to favour the Labour Party in 1945, arouse much protest. Attention focuses on policies and individuals (Chamberlain, Churchill, Cripps, Beveridge, Bevin) rather than on parties. The feeling that Parliament really controls events, and that sensational changes are to be expected when a new government comes in, has been gradually fading ever since the first Labour government in 1923.

In spite of many subdivisions, Britain has in effect only two political parties, the Conservative Party and the Labour Party, which between them broadly represent the main interests of the nation. But during the last twenty years the tendency of these two parties has been to resemble one another more and more. Everyone knows in advance that any government, whatever its political principles may be, can be relied upon not to do certain things. Thus, no Conservative government will ever revert to what would have been called Conservatism in the nineteenth century. No Socialist government will massacre the propertied class, nor even expropriate them without compensation. A good recent example of the changing temper of politics was the reception given to the Beveridge Report. Thirty years ago any Conservative would have denounced this as State charity, while most Socialists would have rejected it as a capitalist bribe. In 1944 the only discussion that arose was as to whether it would be adopted in whole or in part. This blurring of party distinctions is happening in almost all countries, partly because everywhere, except, perhaps, in the U.S.A., the drift is towards a planned economy, partly because in an age of power politics national survival is felt to be more important than class warfare. But Britain has certain peculiarities resulting from its being both a small island and the centre of an Empire. To begin with, given the present economic system, Britain's prosperity depends partly on the Empire, while all Left parties are theoretically anti-imperialist. Politicians of the Left are therefore aware—or have recently become aware —that once in power they choose between abandoning some of their principles or lowering the English standard of living. Secondly, it is impossible for Britain to go through the kind of revolutionary process that the U.S.S.R. went through. It is too small, too highly organised, too dependent on imported food. Civil war in England would mean starvation or conquest by some foreign power, or both. Thirdly and most important of all, civil war is not *morally* possible in England. In any circumstances that we can foresee, the proletariat of Hammersmith will not arise and massacre the *bourgeoisie* of Kensington: they are not different enough. Even the most drastic changes will have to happen peacefully and with a show of legality, and everyone except the "lunatic fringes" of the various political parties is aware of this.

These facts make up the background of the English political outlook. The great mass of the people want profound changes, but they do not want violence. They want to preserve their own standard of living, and at the same time they want to feel that they are not exploiting less fortunate peoples. If you issued a questionnaire to the whole nation, asking, "What do you want from politics?", the answer would be much the same in the overwhelming majority of cases. Substantially it would be: "Economic security, a foreign policy which will ensure peace, more social equality, and a settlement with India." Of these, the first is by far the most important, unemployment being an even greater nightmare than war. But few people would think it necessary to mention either capitalism or socialism. Neither word has much emotional appeal. No one's heart beats faster at the thought of nationalising the Bank of England: on the other hand, the old line of talk about sturdy individualism and the sacred rights of property is no longer swallowed by the masses. They know it is not true that "there's plenty of room at the top," and in any case most of them don't want to get to the top: they want steady jobs and a fair deal for their children.

During the last few years, owing to the social frictions arising out of the war, discontent with the obvious inefficiency of old-style capitalism, and admiration for Soviet Russia, public opinion has moved considerably to the Left, but without growing more doctrinaire or markedly bitterer. None of the political parties which call themselves revolutionary have seriously increased their following. There are about half a dozen of these parties, but their combined membership, even if one counts the remnants of Mosley's Blackshirts, would probably not amount to 150,000. The most important of them is the Communist Party, but even the Communist Party, after twenty-five years of existence, must be held to have failed. Although it has had considerable influence at moments when circumstances favoured it, it has never shown signs of growing into a mass party of the kind that exists in France or used to exist in pre-Hitler Germany.

Over a long period of years, Communist Party membership has gone up or down in response to the changes in Russian foreign policy. When the U.S.S.R. is on good terms with Britain, the British Communists follow a "moderate" line hardly distinguishable from that of the Labour Party, and their membership swells to some scores of thousands. When British and Russian policy diverge, the Communists revert to a "revolutionary" line and membership slumps again. They can, in fact, only get themselves a worthwhile following by abandoning their essential objectives. The various other Marxist parties, all of them claiming to be the true and uncorrupted successors of Lenin, are in an even more hopeless position. The average Englishman is unable to grasp their doctrines and uninterested in their grievances. And in England the conspiratorial mentality which has been developed in police-ridden European countries is a great handicap. English people in large numbers will not accept any creed whose dominant notes are hatred and illegality. The ruthless ideologies of the Continent—not merely communism and fascism, but anarchism, Trotskyism, and even ultramontane Catholicism—are accepted in their pure form only by the intelligentsia, who constitute a sort of island of bigotry amid the general vagueness. It is significant that English revolutionary writers are obliged

THE CAFÉ
Oil painting by Graham Bell, 1911–1943

to use a bastard vocabulary whose key phrases are mostly translations.
There are no native English words for most of the concepts they are dealing
with. Even the word "proletarian," for instance, is not English and the
great majority of English people do not know what it means. It is generally
used, if at all, to mean simply "poor." But even so it is given a social

rather than an economic slant and most people would tell you that a black-smith or a cobbler is a proletarian and that a bank clerk is not. As for the word *"bourgeois,"* it is used almost exclusively by people who are of *bourgeois* origin themselves. The only genuinely popular use of the word is as a printer's term. It is then, as one might expect, anglicised and pronounced "boorjoyce."

But there is one abstract political term which is fairly widely used and has a loose but well-understood meaning attached to it. This is the word "democracy." In a way, the English people do feel that they live in a democratic country. Not that anyone is so stupid as to take this in a literal sense. If democracy means either popular rule or social equality, it is clear that Britain is not democratic. It is, however, democratic in the secondary sense which has attached itself to that word since the rise of Hitler. To begin with, minorities have some power of making themselves heard. But more than this, public opinion cannot be disregarded when it chooses to express itself. It may have to work in indirect ways, by strikes, demonstrations and letters to the newspapers, but it can and visibly does affect government policy. A British government may be unjust, but it cannot be quite arbitrary. It cannot do the kind of thing that a totalitarian government does as a matter of course. One example out of the thousands that might be chosen is the German attack on the U.S.S.R. The significant thing is not that this was made without a declaration of war—that was natural enough—but that it was made without any propaganda build-up beforehand. The German people woke up to find themselves at war with a country that they had been ostensibly on friendly terms with on the previous evening. Our own government would not dare to do such a thing, and the English people are fairly well aware of this. English political thinking is much governed by the word "They." "They" are the higher-ups, the mysterious powers who do things to you against your will. But there is a widespread feeling that "They," though tyrannical, are not omni-potent. "They" will respond to pressure if you take the trouble to apply it: "They" are even removable. And with all their political ignorance the English people will often show surprising sensitiveness when some small incident seems to show that "They" are overstepping the mark. Hence, in the midst of seeming apathy, the sudden fuss every now and then over a rigged by-election or a too-Cromwellian handling of Parliament.

One thing that is extremely difficult to be certain about is the persistence in England of monarchist sentiment. There cannot be much doubt that at any rate in the south of England it was strong and genuine until the death of King George V. The popular response to the Silver Jubilee in 1935 took the authorities by surprise, and the celebrations had to be prolonged for an extra week. At normal times it is only the richer classes who are overtly royalist: in the West End of London, for instance, people stand to attention for "God Save the King" at the end of a picture show, whereas

PUB IN CANNING TOWN
Oil painting by Henry Lamb, 1928

in the poorer quarters they walk out. But the affection shown for George V
at the Silver Jubilee was obviously genuine, and it was even possible to see
in it the survival, or recrudescence, of an idea almost as old as history, the
idea of the King and the common people being in a sort of alliance against
the upper classes; for example, some of the London slum streets bore

during the Jubilee the rather servile slogan "Poor but Loyal." Other slogans, however, coupled loyalty to the King with hostility to the landlord, such as "Long Live the King. Down With the Landlord," or more often, "No Landlords Wanted" or "Landlords Keep Away." It is too early to say whether royalist sentiment was killed outright by the Abdication, but unquestionably the Abdication dealt it a serious blow. Over the past four hundred years it has waxed or waned according to circumstances. Queen Victoria, for instance, was decidedly unpopular during part of her reign, and in the first quarter of the nineteenth century public interest in the Royal Family was not nearly as strong as it was a hundred years later. At this moment the mass of the English people are probably mildly republican. But it may well be that another long reign, similar to that of George V, would revive royalist feeling and make it—as it was between roughly 1880 and 1936—an appreciable factor in politics.

THE ENGLISH CLASS SYSTEM

IN time of war the English class system is the enemy propagandist's best argument. To Dr. Goebbels's charge that England is still "two nations," the only truthful answer would have been that she is in fact three nations. But the peculiarity of English class distinctions is not that they are unjust—for after all, wealth and poverty exist side by side in almost all countries—but that they are anachronistic. They do not exactly correspond to economic distinctions, and what is essentially an industrial and capitalist country is haunted by the ghost of a caste system.

It is usual to classify modern society under three headings: the upper class, or *bourgeoisie*, the middle class, or *petite bourgeoisie*, and the working class, or proletariat. This roughly fits the facts, but one can draw no useful inference from it unless one takes account of the subdivisions within the various classes and realises how deeply the whole English outlook is coloured by romanticism and sheer snobbishness.

England is one of the last remaining countries to cling to the outward forms of feudalism. Titles are maintained and new ones are constantly created, and the House of Lords, consisting mainly of hereditary peers, has real powers. At the same time England has no real aristocracy. The race difference on which aristocratic rule is usually founded was disappearing by the end of the Middle Ages, and the famous medieval families have almost completely vanished. The so-called old families are those that grew rich in the sixteenth, seventeenth, and eighteenth centuries. Moreover, the notion that nobility exists in its own right, that you can be a nobleman even if you are poor, was already dying out in the age of Elizabeth, a fact commented on by Shakespeare. And yet, curiously enough, the English ruling

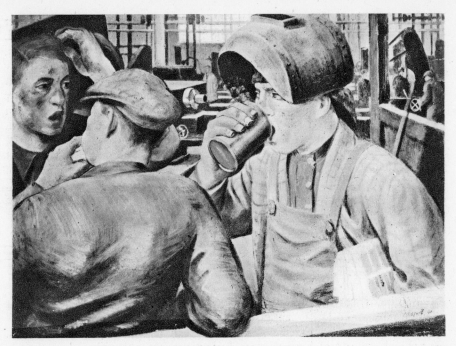

SNACK TIME IN A FACTORY
Oil painting by Vivian Pitchforth, 1940

class has never developed into a *bourgeoisie* plain and simple. It has never become purely urban or frankly commercial. The ambition to be a country gentleman, to own and administer land and draw at least a part of your income from rent, has survived every change. So it comes that each new wave of parvenus, instead of simply replacing the existing ruling class, has adopted its habits, intermarried with it, and, after a generation or two, become indistinguishable from it.

The basic reason for this may perhaps be that England is very small and has an equable climate and pleasantly varied scenery. It is almost impossible in England, and not easy even in Scotland, to be more than twenty miles from a town. Rural life is less inherently boorish than it is in bigger countries with colder winters. And the comparative integrity of the British ruling class—for when all is said and done they have not behaved so contemptibly as their European opposite numbers—is probably bound up with their idea of themselves as feudal landowners. This outlook is shared by considerable sections of the middle class. Nearly everyone who can afford to do so sets up as a country gentleman, or at least makes some effort in that direction. The manor-house with its park and its walled gardens reappears in reduced form in the stockbroker's week-end cottage, in the suburban villa with its lawn and herbaceous border, perhaps even in the potted nasturtiums on the window-sill of the Bayswater flat. This widespread day-dream is undoubtedly snobbish, it has tended to stabilise class distinctions and has helped to prevent the modernisation of English agriculture: but it is mixed up with a kind of idealism, a feeling that style and tradition are more important than money.

Within the middle class there is a sharp division, cultural and not financial, between those who aim at gentility and those who do not. According to the usual classification, everyone between the capitalist and the weekly wage-earner can be lumped together as *"petite bourgeoisie."* This means that the Harley Street physician, the army officer, the grocer, the farmer, the senior civil servant, the solicitor, the clergyman, the schoolmaster, the bank manager, the speculative builder, and the fisherman who owns his own boat, are all in the same class. But no one in England feels them to belong to the same class, and the distinction between them is not a distinction of income but of accent, manners and, to some extent, outlook. Anyone who pays any attention to class differences at all would regard an army officer with £1,000 a year as socially superior to a shopkeeper with £2,000 a year. Even within the upper class a similar distinction holds good, the titled person being almost always more deferred to than an untitled person of larger income. Middle-class people are really graded according to their degree of resemblance to the aristocracy: professional men, senior officials, officers in the fighting services, university lecturers, clergymen, even the literary and scientific intelligentsia, rank higher than business men, though on the whole they earn less. It is a peculiarity of this class that their largest item of expenditure is education. Whereas a successful tradesman will send his son to the local grammar school, a clergyman with half his income will underfeed himself for years in order to send his son to a public school, although he knows that he will get no direct return for the money he spends.

There is, however, another noticeable division in the middle class. The old distinction was between the man who is "a gentleman" and the man who is "not a gentleman." In the last thirty years, however, the demands of modern industry, and the technical schools and provincial universities, have brought into being a new kind of man, middle class in income and to some extent in habits, but not much interested in his own social status. People like radio engineers and industrial chemists, whose education has not been of a kind to give them any reverence for the past, and who tend to live in blocks of flats or housing-estates where the old social pattern has broken down, are the most nearly classless beings that England possesses. They are an important section of society, because their numbers are constantly growing. The war, for instance, made necessary the formation of an enormous air force, and so you got thousands of young men of working-class origin graduating into the technical middle class by way of the R.A.F. Any serious reorganisation of industry now will have similar effects. And the characteristic outlook of the technicians is already spreading among the older strata of the middle class. One symptom of this is that intermarriage within the middle class is freer than it used to be. Another is the increasing unwillingness of people below the £2,000 a year level to bankrupt themselves in the name of education.

Another series of changes, probably dating from the Education Bill of 1871, is occurring in the working class. One cannot altogether acquit the English working class either of snobbishness or of servility. To begin with there is a fairly sharp distinction between the better-paid working class and the very poor. Even in socialist literature it is common to find contemptuous references to slum-dwellers (the German word *lumpenproletariat* is much used), and imported labourers with low standards of living, such as the Irish, are greatly looked down on. There is also, probably, more disposition to accept class distinctions as permanent, and even to accept the upper classes as natural leaders, than survives in most countries. It is significant that in the moment of disaster the man best able to unite the nation was Churchill, a Conservative of aristocratic origins. The word "Sir" is much used in England, and the man of obviously upper-class appearance can usually get more than his fair share of deference from commissionaires, ticket-collectors, policemen, and the like. It is this aspect of English life that seems most shocking to visitors from America and the Dominions. And the tendency towards servility probably did not decrease in the twenty years between the two wars: it may even have increased, owing chiefly to unemployment.

But snobbishness is never quite separable from idealism. The tendency to give the upper classes more than their due is mixed up with a respect for good manners and something vaguely describable as culture. In the South of England, at any rate, it is unquestionable that most working-class people want to resemble the upper classes in manners and habits. The traditional attitude of looking down on the upper classes as effeminate and "la-di-dah" survives best in the heavy-industry areas. Hostile nicknames like "toff" and "swell" have almost disappeared, and even the *Daily Worker* displays advertisements for "High-class Gentleman's Tailor." Above all, throughout southern England there is almost general uneasiness about the Cockney accent. In Scotland and northern England snobbishness about the local accents does exist, but it is not nearly so strong or widespread. Many a Yorkshireman definitely prides himself on his broad U's and narrow A's, and will defend them on linguistic grounds. In London there are still people who say "fice" instead of "face," but there is probably no one who regards "fice" as superior. Even a person who claims to despise the *bourgeoisie* and all its ways will still take care that his children grow up pronouncing their aitches.

But side by side with this there has gone a considerable growth of political consciousness and an increasing impatience with class privilege.

Over a period of twenty or thirty years the working class has grown politically more hostile to the upper class, culturally less hostile. There is nothing incongruous in this: both tendencies are symptoms of the levelling of manners which results from machine civilisation and which makes the English class system more and more of an anachronism.

The obvious class differences still surviving in England astonish foreign observers, but they are far less marked, and far less real, than they were thirty years ago. People of different social origins, thrown together during the war in the armed forces, or in factories or offices, or as firewatchers and Home Guards, were able to mingle more easily than they did in the 1914-18 war. It is worth listing the various influences which—mechanically, as it were—tend to make Englishmen of all classes less and less different from one another.

First of all, the improvement in industrial technique. Every year less and less people are engaged in heavy manual labour which keeps them constantly tired and, by hypertrophying certain muscles, gives them a distinctive carriage. Secondly, improvements in housing. Between the two wars rehousing was done mostly by the local authorities, who have produced a type of house (the council house, with its bathroom, garden, separate kitchen, and indoor w.c.) which is nearer to the stockbroker's villa than it is to the labourer's cottage. Thirdly, the mass production of furniture which in ordinary times can be bought on the hire-purchase system. The effect of this is that the interior of a working-class house resembles that of a middle-class house very much more than it did a generation ago. Fourthly, and perhaps most important of all, the mass production of cheap clothes. Thirty years ago the social status of nearly everyone in England could be determined from his appearance, even at two hundred yards' distance. The working classes all wore ready-made clothes, and the ready-made clothes were not only ill-fitting but usually followed the upper-class fashions of ten or fifteen years earlier. The cloth cap was practically a badge of status. It was universal among the working class, while the upper classes only wore it for golf and shooting. This state of affairs is rapidly changing. Ready-made clothes now follow the fashions closely, they are made in many different fittings to suit every kind of figure, and even when they are of very cheap cloth they are superficially not very different from expensive clothes. The result it that it grows harder every year, especially in the case of women, to determine social status at a glance.

Mass-produced literature and amusements have the same effect. Radio programmes, for instance, are necessarily the same for everybody. Films, though often extremely reactionary in their implied outlook, have to appeal to a public of millions and therefore have to avoid stirring up class antagonisms. So also with some of the big-circulation newspapers. The *Daily Express,* for instance, draws its readers from all strata of the population. So also with some of the periodicals that have appeared in the past dozen years. *Punch* is obviously a middle- and upper-class paper, but *Picture Post* is not

MINERS AT THE PIT HEAD
Water colour by Henry Moore, 1942

aimed at any particular class. And lending libraries and very cheap books, such as the Penguins, popularise the habit of reading and probably have a levelling effect on literary taste. Even taste in food tends to grow more uniform owing to the multiplication of cheap but fairly smart restaurants such as those of Messrs. Lyons.

We are not justified in assuming that class distinctions are actually disappearing. The essential structure of England is still almost what it was in the nineteenth century. But real differences between man and man are obviously diminishing, and this fact is grasped and even welcomed by people who only a few years ago were clinging desperately to their social prestige.

Whatever may be the ultimate fate of the very rich, the tendency of the working class and the middle class is evidently to merge. It may happen quickly or slowly, according to circumstances. It was accelerated by the war, and another ten years of all-round rationing, utility clothes, high income tax, and compulsory national service may finish the process once and for all. The final effects of this we cannot foresee. There are observers, both native and foreign, who believe that the fairly large amount of individual freedom that is enjoyed in England depends on having a well-defined class system. Liberty, according to some, is incompatible with equality. But at least it is certain that the present drift *is* towards greater social equality, and that that is what the great mass of the English people desire.

31

THE ENGLISH LANGUAGE

THE English language has two outstanding characteristics to which most of its minor oddities can be finally traced. These characteristics are a very large vocabulary and simplicity of grammar.

If it is not the largest in the world, the English vocabulary is certainly among the largest. English is really two languages, Anglo-Saxon and Norman-French, and during the last three centuries it has been reinforced on an enormous scale by new words deliberately created from Latin and Greek roots. But in addition the vocabulary is made much larger than it appears by the practice of turning one part of speech into another. For example, almost any noun can be used as a verb: this in effect gives an extra range of verbs, so that you have *knife* as well as *stab*, *school* as well as *teach*, *fire* as well as *burn*, and so on. Then again, certain verbs can be given as many as twenty different meanings simply by adding prepositions to them. (Examples are *get out of, get up, give out, take over*.) Verbs can also change into nouns with considerable freedom, and by the use of affixes such as *-y, -ful, -like*, any noun can be turned into an adjective. More freely than in most languages, verbs and adjectives can be turned into their opposites by means of the prefix *un-*. And adjectives can be made more emphatic or given a new twist by tying a noun to them; for example, *lily-white, sky-blue, coal-black, iron-hard*, etc.

But English is also, and to an unnecessary extent, a borrowing language. It readily takes over any foreign word that seems to fill a need, often altering the meaning in doing so. A recent example is the word *blitz*. As a verb this word did not appear in print till late in 1940, but it has already become part of the language. Other examples from the vast armoury of borrowed words are *garage, charabanc, alias, alibi, steppe, thug, role, menu, lasso, rendezvous, chemise*. It will be noticed that in most cases an English equivalent exists already, so that borrowing adds to the already large stock of synonyms.

English grammar is simple. The language is almost completely uninflected, a peculiarity which marks it off from almost all languages west of China. Any regular English verb has only three inflections, the third person singular, the present participle, and the past participle. Thus, for instance, the verb *to kill* consists of *kill, kills, killing, killed*, and that is all. There is, of course, a great wealth of tenses, very much subtilised in meaning, but these are made by the use of auxiliaries which themselves barely inflect. *May, might, shall, will, should, would* do not inflect at all, except in the obsolete second person singular. The upshot is that every person in every tense of such a verb as *to kill* can be expressed in only about thirty words including the pronouns, or about forty if one includes the second person singular. The corresponding number in, for instance, French would be somewhere near two hundred. And in English there is

FOOTBALL EDITION
Scene near the Station, Poole, Dorset
Oil painting by Henry Lamb, 1926

SATURDAY AFTERNOON
A Derbyshire Village
Oil painting by L. S. Lowry, 1943

the added advantage that the auxiliaries which are used to make the tenses are the same in every case.

There is no such thing in English as declension of nouns, and there is no gender. Nor are there many irregular plurals or comparatives. Moreover, the tendency is always towards greater simplicity, both in grammar and syntax. Long sentences with dependent clauses grow more and more unpopular, irregular but time-saving formations such as the "American subjunctive" (*it is necessary that you go* instead of *it is necessary that you should go*) gain ground, and difficult rules, such as the difference between *shall* and *will*, or *that* and *which*, are more and more ignored. If it continues to develop along its present lines English will ultimately have more in common with the uninflected languages of East Asia than with the languages of Europe.

The greatest quality of English is its enormous range not only of meaning but of *tone*. It is capable of endless subtleties, and of everything from the most high-flown rhetoric to the most brutal coarseness. On the other hand, its lack of grammar makes it easily compressible. It is the language of lyric poetry, and also of headlines. On its lower levels it is very easy to learn, in spite of its irrational spelling. It can also for international purposes be reduced to very simple pidgin dialects, ranging from Basic to the "Bêche-de-mer" English used in the South Pacific. It is therefore well suited to be a world lingua franca, and it has in fact spread more widely than any other language.

But there are also great disadvantages, or at least great dangers, in speaking English as one's native tongue. To begin with, as was pointed out earlier in this book, the English are very poor linguists. Their own language is grammatically so simple that unless they have gone through the discipline of learning a foreign language in childhood, they are often quite unable to grasp what is meant by gender, person, and case. A completely illiterate Indian will pick up English far faster than a British soldier will pick up Hindustani. Nearly five million Indians are literate in English and millions more speak it in a debased form. There are some tens of thousands of Indians who speak English as nearly as possible perfectly; yet the number of Englishmen speaking any Indian language perfectly would not amount to more than a few scores. But the great weakness of English is its capacity for debasement. Just because it is so easy to use, it is easy to use *badly*.

To write or even to speak English is not a science but an art. There are no reliable rules: there is only the general principle that concrete words are better than abstract ones, and that the shortest way of saying anything is always the best. Mere correctness is no guarantee whatever of good writing. A sentence like "an enjoyable time was had by all present" is perfectly correct English, and so is the unintelligible mess of words on an income-tax return. Whoever writes English is involved in a struggle that

33

never lets up even for a sentence. He is struggling against vagueness, against obscurity, against the lure of the decorative adjective, against the encroachment of Latin and Greek, and, above all, against the worn-out phrases and dead metaphors with which the language is cluttered up. In speaking, these dangers are more easily avoided, but spoken English differs from written English more sharply than is the case in most languages. In the spoken tongue every word that can be omitted is omitted, every possible abbreviation is used. Meaning is conveyed quite largely by emphasis, though curiously enough the English do not gesticulate, as one might reasonably expect them to do. A sentence like *No, I don't mean that one, I mean that one* is perfectly intelligible when spoken aloud, even without a gesture. But spoken English, when it tries to be dignified and logical, usually takes on the vices of written English, as you can see by spending half an hour either in the House of Commons or at the Marble Arch.

English is peculiarly subject to jargons. Doctors, scientists, business men, officials, sportsmen, economists, and political theorists all have their characteristic perversion of the language, which can be studied in the appropriate magazines from the *Lancet* to the *Labour Monthly*. But probably the deadliest enemy of good English is what is called "standard English." This dreary dialect, the language of leading articles, White Papers, political speeches, and B.B.C. news bulletins, is undoubtedly spreading: it is spreading downwards in the social scale, and outwards into the spoken language. Its characteristic is its reliance on ready-made phrases—*in due course, take the earliest opportunity, warm appreciation, deepest regret, explore every avenue, ring the changes, take up the cudgels, legitimate assumption, the answer is in the affirmative*, etc. etc.—which may once have been fresh and vivid, but have now become mere thought-saving devices, having the same relation to living English as a crutch has to a leg. Anyone preparing a broadcast or writing a letter to *The Times* adopts this kind of language almost instinctively, and it infects the spoken tongue as well. So much has our language been weakened that the imbecile chatter in Swift's essay on *Polite Conversation* (a satire on the upper-class talk of Swift's own day) would actually be rather a good conversation by modern standards.

This temporary decadence of the English language is due, like so much else, to our anachronistic class system. "Educated" English has grown anæmic because for long past it has not been reinvigorated from below. The people likeliest to use simple concrete language, and to think of metaphors that really call up a visual image, are those who are in contact with physical reality. A useful word like *bottleneck*, for instance, would be most likely to occur to someone used to dealing with conveyor belts: or again, the expressive military phrase *to winkle out* implies acquaintance both with winkles and with machine-gun nests. And the vitality of English depends on a steady supply of images of this kind. It follows that language, at any

AN ENGLISHMAN
Self-portrait in oil by George Belcher, 1946

rate the English language, suffers when the educated classes lose touch with the manual workers. As things are at present, nearly every English-man, whatever his origins, feels the working-class manner of speech, and even working-class idioms, to be inferior. Cockney, the most widespread dialect, is the most despised of all. Any word or usage that is supposedly Cockney is looked on as vulgar, even when, as is sometimes the case, it is merely an archaism. An example is *ain't*, which is now abandoned in favour of the much weaker form *aren't*. But *ain't* was good enough English eighty years ago, and Queen Victoria would have said *ain't*.

During the past forty years, and especially the past dozen years, English has borrowed largely from American, while America has shown no tendency to borrow from English. The reason for this is partly political.

"AUNTIE"
Oil painting by B. Fleetwood-Walker, 1946

Anti-British feeling in the United States is far stronger than anti-American feeling in England, and most Americans dislike using a word or phrase which they know to be British. But American has gained a footing in England partly because of the vivid, almost poetic quality of its slang, partly because certain American usages (for instance, the formation of verbs by adding *-ise* to a noun) save time, and most of all because one can adopt an American word without crossing a class barrier. From the English point of view American words have no class label. This applies even to thieves' slang. Words like *stooge* and *stool-pigeon* are considered much less vulgar than words like *nark* and *split*. Even a very snobbish English person would probably not mind calling a policeman a *cop*, which is American, but he would object to calling him a *copper*, which is working-

YOUNG GIRL READING
Oil painting by Patricia Preece

class English. To the working classes, on the other hand, the use of Americanisms is a way of escaping from Cockney without adopting the B.B.C. dialect, which they instinctively dislike and cannot easily master. Hence, especially in the big towns, working-class children now use American slang from the moment that they learn to talk. And there is a noticeable tendency to use American words even when they are not slang and when an English equivalent already exists: for instance, *car* for *tram*, *escalator* for *moving staircase, automobile* for *motor-car*.

This process will probably continue for some time. One cannot check it simply by protesting against it, and in any case many American words and expressions are well worth adopting. Some are necessary neologisms, others (for instance, *fall* for *autumn*) are old words which we ought never

37

to have dropped. But it ought to be realised that on the whole American is a bad influence and has already had a debasing effect.

To begin with, American has some of the vices of English in an exaggerated form. The interchangeability of different parts of speech has been carried further, the distinction between transitive and intransitive verbs tends to break down, and many words are used which have no meaning whatever. For example, whereas English alters the meaning of a verb by tacking a preposition on to it, the American tendency is to burden every verb with a preposition that adds nothing to its meaning (*win out, lose out, face up to,* etc.). On the other hand, American has broken more completely than English with the past and with literary traditions. It not only produces words like *beautician, moronic,* and *sexualise,* but often replaces strong primary words by feeble euphemisms. For instance, many Americans seem to regard the word *death* and various words that go with it (*corpse, coffin, shroud*) as almost unmentionable. But above all, to adopt the American language wholeheartedly would probably mean a huge loss of vocabulary. For though American produces vivid and witty turns of speech, it is terribly poor in names for natural objects and localities. Even the streets in American cities are usually known by numbers instead of names. If we really intended to model our language upon American we should have, for instance, to lump the lady-bird, the daddy-long-legs, the sawfly, the water-boatman, the cockchafer, the cricket, the death-watch beetle and scores of other insects all together under the inexpressive name of *bug.* We should lose the poetic names of our wild flowers, and also, probably, our habit of giving individual names to every street, pub, field, lane, and hillock. In so far as American is adopted, that is the tendency. Those who take their language from the films, or from papers such as *Life* and *Time,* always prefer the slick time-saving word to the one with a history behind it. As to accent, it is doubtful whether the American accent has the superiority which it is now fashionable to claim for it. The "educated" English accent, a product of the last thirty years, is undoubtedly very bad and is likely to be abandoned, but the average English person probably speaks as clearly as the average American. Most English people blur their vowel sounds, but most Americans swallow their consonants. Many Americans pronounce, for instance, *water* as though it had no T in it, or even as though it had no consonant in it at all, except the w. On the whole we are justified in regarding the American language with suspicion. We ought to be ready to borrow its best words, but we ought not to let it modify the actual structure of our language.

However, there is no chance of resisting the American influence unless we can put new life into English itself. And it is difficult to do this while words and idioms are prevented from circulating freely among all sections of the population. English people of all classes now find it natural to express incredulity by the American slang phrase *sez you.* Many would

AN ENGLISH SAILOR
Oil painting by William Dring, 1942

even tell you in good faith that *sez you* has no English equivalent. Actually it has a whole string of them—for instance, *not half, I don't think, come off it, less of it, and then you wake up,* or simply *garn.* But most of these would be considered vulgar: you would never find an expression like *not half* in a *Times* leader, for instance. And on the other hand, many necessary abstract words, especially words of Latin origin, are rejected by the working class because they sound public-schoolish, "tony," and effeminate. Language ought to be the joint creation of poets and manual workers, and in modern England it is difficult for these two classes to meet. When they can do so again—as, in a different way, they could in the feudal past—English may show more clearly than at present its kinship with the language of Shakespeare and Defoe.

39

THE FUTURE OF THE ENGLISH PEOPLE

THIS is not a book about foreign politics, but if one is to speak of the future of the English people, one must start by considering what kind of world they will probably be living in and what special part they can play in it.

Nations do not often die out, and the English people will still be in existence a hundred years hence, whatever has happened in the meantime. But if Britain is to survive as what is called a "great" nation, playing an important and useful part in the world's affairs, one must take certain things as assured. One must assume that Britain will remain on good terms with Russia and Europe, will keep its special links with America and the Dominions, and will solve the problem of India in some amicable way. That is perhaps a great deal to assume, but without it there is not much hope for civilisation as a whole, and still less for Britain itself. If the savage international struggle of the last twenty years continues, there will only be room in the world for two or three great powers, and in the long run Britain will not be one of them. It has not either the population or the resources. In a world of power politics the English would ultimately dwindle to a satellite people, and the special thing that it is in their power to contribute might be lost.

But what is the special thing that they could contribute? The outstanding and—by contemporary standards—highly original quality of the English is their habit of *not killing one another*. Putting aside the "model" small states, which are in an exceptional position, England is the only European country where internal politics are conducted in a more or less humane and decent manner. It is—and this was true long before the rise of fascism—the only country where armed men do not prowl the streets and no one is frightened of the secret police. And the whole British Empire, with all its crying abuses, its stagnation in one place and exploitation in another, at least has the merit of being internally peaceful. It has always been able to get along with a very small number of armed men, although it contains a quarter of the population of the earth. Between the wars its total armed forces amounted to about 600,000 men, of whom a third were Indians. At the outbreak of war the entire Empire was able to mobilise about a million trained men. Almost as many could have been mobilised by, say, Rumania. The English are probably more capable than most peoples of making revolutionary changes without bloodshed. In England, if anywhere, it would be possible to abolish poverty without destroying liberty. If the English took the trouble to make their own democracy work, they would become the political leaders of western Europe, and probably of some other parts of the world as well. They would provide the much-needed alternative to Russian authoritarianism on the one hand and American materialism on the other.

'THE GODS'
The Gallery at a London Theatre
Oil painting by Sydney Seymour-Lucas, 1942

INDUSTRIAL LANDSCAPE

The Great North Road at Castleford. South Yorkshire

But to play a leading part the English have got to know what they are doing, and they have got to retain their vitality. For this, certain developments are needed within the next decade. These are a rising birthrate, more social equality, less centralisation and more respect for the intellect.

There was a small rise in the birthrate during the war years, but that is probably of no significance, and the general curve is downwards. The position is not quite so desperate as it is sometimes said to be, but it can only be put right if the curve not only rises sharply, but does so within ten or at most twenty years. Otherwise the population will not only fall, but, what is worse, will consist predominantly of middle-aged people. If that point is reached, the decline may never be retrievable.

At bottom, the causes of the dwindled birthrate are economic. It is nonsense to say that it has happened because English people do not care for children. In the early nineteenth century they had an extremely high birthrate, and they also had an attitude towards children which now seems to us unbelievably callous. With very little public disapproval, children as young as six were sold into the mines and factories, and the death of a child, the most shocking event that modern people are able to imagine, was looked on as a very minor tragedy. In a sense it is true that modern English people have small families because they are too fond of children. They feel that it is wrong to bring a child into the world unless you are completely certain of being able to provide for him, and at a level not lower than your own. For the last fifty years, to have a big family has meant that your children must wear poorer clothes than others in the same group, must have less food and less attention, and probably must go to work earlier. This held good for all classes except the very rich and the unemployed. No doubt the dearth of babies is partly due to the competing attraction of cars and radios, but its main cause is a typically English mixture of snobbishness and altruism.

The philoprogenitive instinct will probably return when fairly large families are already the rule, but the first steps towards this must be economic ones. Half-hearted family allowances will not do the trick, especially when there is a severe housing shortage, as there is now. People should be better off for having children, just as they are in a peasant community, instead of being financially crippled, as they are in ours. Any government, by a few strokes of the pen, could make childlessness as unbearable an economic burden as a big family is now: but no government has chosen to do so, because of the ignorant idea that a bigger population means more unemployed. Far more drastically than anyone has proposed hitherto, taxation will have to be graded so as to encourage child-bearing and to save women with young children from being obliged to work outside the home. And this involves readjustment of rents, better public service in the matter of nursery schools and playing grounds, and the building of bigger and more convenient houses. It also probably involves the extension and improvement

41

of free education, so that the middle-class family shall not, as at present, be crushed out of existence by impossibly high school fees.

The economic adjustments must come first, but a change of outlook is also needed. In the England of the last thirty years it has seemed all too natural that blocks of flats should refuse tenants with children, that parks and squares should be railed off to keep the children out of them, that abortion, theoretically illegal, should be looked on as a peccadillo, and that the main aim of commercial advertising should be to popularise the idea of "having a good time" and staying young as long as possible. Even the cult of animals, fostered by the newspapers, has probably done its bit towards reducing the birthrate. Nor have the public authorities seriously interested themselves in this question till very recently. Britain to-day has a million and a half less children than in 1914, and a million and a half more dogs. Yet even now, when the government designs a prefabricated house, it produces a house with only two bedrooms—with room, that is to say, for two children at the most. When one considers the history of the years between the wars, it is perhaps surprising that the birthrate has not dropped more catastrophically than it has. But it is not likely to rise to the replacement level until those in power, as well as the ordinary people in the street, come to feel that children matter more than money.

The English are probably less irked by class distinctions, more tolerant of privilege and of absurdities like titles, than most peoples. There is nevertheless, as I have pointed out earlier, a growing wish for greater equality and a tendency, below the £2,000 a year level, for surface differences between class and class to disappear. At present this is happening only mechanically and quite largely as a result of the war. The question is how it can be speeded up. For even the change-over to a centralised economy, which, except, possibly, in the United States, is happening in all countries under one name or another, does of itself guarantee greater equality between man and man. Once civilisation has reached a fairly high technical level, class distinctions are an obvious evil. They not only lead great numbers of people to waste their lives in the pursuit of social prestige, but they also cause an immense wastage of talent. In England it is not merely the ownership of property that is concentrated in a few hands. It is also the case that all power, administrative as well as financial, belongs to a single class, Except for a handful of "self-made men" and Labour politicians, those who control our destinies are the product of about a dozen public schools and two universities. A nation is using its capacities to the full when any man can get any job that he is fit for. One has only to think of some of the people who have held vitally important jobs during the past twenty years, and to wonder what would have happened to them if they had been born into the working class, to see that this is not the case in England.

Moreover, class distinctions are a constant drain on morale, in peace as well as in war. And the more conscious, the better educated, the mass of

A ROADMAN, EARLY MORNING
Oil painting by George Brownrigg, 1937

the people become, the more this is so. The word "They," the universal
feeling that "They" hold all the power and make all the decisions, and that
"They" can only be influenced in indirect and uncertain ways, is a great
handicap in England. In 1940 "They" showed a marked tendency to give
place to "We," and it is time that it did so permanently. Three measures
are obviously necessary, and they would begin to produce their effect
within a few years.

The first is a scaling-up and scaling-down of incomes. The glaring
inequality of wealth that existed in England before the war must not be
allowed to recur. Above a certain point—which should bear a fixed
relation to the lowest current wage—all income should be taxed out of
existence. In theory, at any rate, this has happened already, with
beneficial results. The second necessary measure is greater democracy in
education. A completely unified system of education is probably not desirable. Some adolescents benefit by higher education, others do not, there

43

is need to differentiate between literary and technical education, and it is better that a few independent experimental schools should remain in existence. But it should be the rule, as it is in some countries already, for all children to attend the same schools up to the age of twelve or at least ten. After that age it becomes necessary to separate the more gifted children from the less gifted, but a uniform educational system for the early years would cut away one of the deepest roots of snobbery.

The third thing that is needed is to remove the class labels from the English language. It is not desirable that all the local accents should disappear, but there should be a manner of speaking that is definitely national and is not merely (like the accent of the B.B.C. announcers) a copy of the mannerisms of the upper classes. This national accent—a modification of Cockney, perhaps, or of one of the northern accents—should be taught as a matter of course to all children alike. After that they could, and in some parts of the country they probably would, revert to the local accent, but they should be able to speak standard English if they wished to. No one should be "branded on the tongue." It should be impossible, as it is in the United States and some European countries, to determine anyone's status from his accent.

We need, too, to be less centralised. English agriculture revived during the war, and the revival may continue, but the English people are still excessively urban in outlook. Culturally, moreover, the country is very much over-centralised. Not only is the whole of Britain in effect governed from London, but the sense of locality—of being, say, an East Anglian or a West Countryman as well as an Englishman—has been much weakened during the past century. The ambition of the farm labourer is usually to get to a town, the provincial intellectual always wants to get to London. In both Scotland and Wales there are nationalist movements, but they are founded on an economic grievance against England rather than on genuine local pride. Nor is there any important literary or artistic movement that is truly independent of London and the university towns.

It is uncertain whether this centralising tendency is completely reversible, but a good deal could be done to check it. Both Scotland and Wales could and should be a great deal more autonomous than they are at present. The provincial universities should be more generously equipped and the provincial press subsidised. (At present nearly the whole of England is "covered" by eight London newspapers. No newspaper with a large circulation, and no first-class magazine, is published outside London.) The problem of getting people, and especially young, spirited people, to stay on the land would be partly solved if farm labourers had better cottages and if country towns were more civilised and cross-country bus services more efficient. Above all, local pride should be stimulated by teaching in the elementary schools. Every child ought as a matter of course to learn something of the history and topography of its own county. People

PLOUGHING
Water colour by Dame Laura Knight, 1942

ought to be proud of their own locality, they ought to feel that its scenery, its architecture and even its cookery are the best in the world. And such feelings, which do exist in some areas of the North but have lapsed throughout the greater part of England, would strengthen national unity rather than weaken it.

It has been suggested earlier that the survival of free speech in England is partly the result of stupidity. The people are not intellectual enough to be heresy-hunters. One does not wish them to grow less tolerant, nor, having seen the results, would one want them to develop the political sophistication that prevailed in pre-Hitler Germany or pre-Pétain France. But the instincts and traditions on which the English rely served them best when they were an exceptionally fortunate people, protected by geography from major disaster. In the twentieth century the narrow interests of the average man, the rather low level of English education, the contempt for "highbrows" and the almost general deadness to æsthetic issues, are serious liabilities.

What the upper classes think about "highbrows" can be judged from the Honours Lists. The upper classes feel titles to be important: yet almost never is any major honour bestowed on anyone describable as an intellectual. With very few exceptions, scientists do not get beyond

45

baronetcies, or literary men beyond knighthoods. But the attitude of the man in the street is no better. He is not troubled by the reflection that England spends hundreds of millions every year on beer and the football pools while scientific research languishes for lack of funds; or that we can afford greyhound tracks innumerable but not even one National Theatre. Between the wars England tolerated newspapers, films, and radio programmes of unheard-of silliness, and these produced further stupefaction in the public, blinding their eyes to vitally important problems. This silliness of the English press is partly artificial, since it arises from the fact that newspapers live off advertisements for consumption goods. During the war the papers grew very much more intelligent without losing their public, and millions of people read papers which they would have rejected as impossibly "highbrow" some years ago. There is, however, not only a low general level of taste, but a widespread unawareness that æsthetic considerations can possibly have any importance. Rehousing and town-planning, for instance, are normally discussed without even a mention of beauty or ugliness. The English are great lovers of flowers, gardening and "nature," but this is merely a part of their vague aspiration towards an agricultural life. In the main they see no objection to "ribbon development" or to the filth and chaos of the industrial towns. They see nothing wrong in scattering the woods with paper bags and filling every pool and stream with tin cans and bicycle frames. And they are all too ready to listen to any journalist who tells them to trust their instincts and despise the "highbrow."

One result of this has been to increase the isolation of the British intelligentsia. English intellectuals, especially the younger ones, are markedly hostile to their own country. Exceptions can, of course, be found, but it is broadly true that anyone who would prefer T. S. Eliot to Alfred Noyes despises England, or thinks that he ought to do so. In "enlightened" circles, to express pro-British sentiments needs considerable moral courage. On the other hand, during the past dozen years there has been a strong tendency to develop a violent nationalistic loyalty to some foreign country, usually Soviet Russia. This must probably have happened in any case, because capitalism in its later phases pushes the literary and even the scientific intellectual into a position where he has security without much responsibility. But the philistinism of the English public alienates the intelligentsia still further. The loss to society is very great. It means that the people whose vision is acutest—the people, for instance, who grasped that Hitler was dangerous ten years before this was discovered by our public men—are hardly able to make contact with the masses and grow less and less interested in English problems.

The English will never develop into a nation of philosophers. They will always prefer instinct to logic, and character to intelligence. But they must get rid of their downright contempt for "cleverness." They cannot

THE FAMILY
Drawing for a sculpture group by Henry Moore, 1944

afford it any longer. They must grow less tolerant of ugliness, and mentally more adventurous. And they must stop despising foreigners. They are Europeans and ought to be aware of it. On the other hand they have special links with the other English-speakers overseas, and special imperial responsibilities, in which they ought to take more interest than they have done during these past twenty years. The intellectual atmosphere of England is already very much livelier than it was. The war scotched if it did not kill certain kinds of folly. But there is still need for a conscious effort at national re-education. The first step towards this is an improvement in elementary education, which involves not only raising the school-leaving age but spending enough money to ensure that elementary schools are adequately staffed and equipped. And there are immense educational possibilities in the radio, the film, and—if it could be freed once and for all from commercial interests—the press.

These, then, appear to be the immediate necessities of the English people. They must breed faster, work harder, and probably live more simply, think more deeply, get rid of their snobbishness and their anachronistic class distinctions, and pay more attention to the world and less to their own backyards. Nearly all of them already love their country, but they must learn to love it intelligently. They must have a clear notion of their own destiny and not listen either to those who tell them that England is finished or to those who tell them that the England of the past can return.

If they can do that they can keep their feet in the post-war world, and if they can keep their feet they can give the example that millions of human beings are waiting for. The world is sick of chaos and it is sick of dictatorship. Of all peoples the English are likeliest to find a way of avoiding both. Except for a small minority they are fully ready for the drastic economic changes that are needed, and at the same time they have no desire either for violent revolution or for foreign conquests. They have known for forty years, perhaps, something that the Germans and the Japanese have only recently learned, and that the Russians and the Americans have yet to learn: they know that it is not possible for any one nation to rule the earth. They want above all things to live at peace, internally and externally. And the great mass of them are probably prepared for the sacrifices that peace entails.

But they will have to take their destiny into their own hands. England can only fulfil its special mission if the ordinary English in the street can somehow get their hands on power. We were told very frequently during the war years that this time, when the danger was over, there should be no lost opportunities, no recurrence of the past. No more stagnation punctuated by wars, no more Rolls-Royces gliding past dole queues, no return to the England of the Distressed Area, the endlessly stewing teapot, the empty pram, and the Giant Panda. We cannot be sure that this promise will be kept. Only we ourselves can make certain that it will come true, and if we do not, no further chance may be given to us. The past thirty years have been a long series of cheques drawn upon the accumulated good will of the English people. That reserve may not be inexhaustible. By the end of another decade it will be finally clear whether England is to survive as a great nation or not. And if the answer is to be "Yes," it is the common people who must make it so.